Between the Shadow and the Rose

selected poems, 2001-2024

Carlos Penela

A Bilingual Edition
English and Galician

OPEN ENDS PRESS

Cover and interior design: David Ter-Avanesyan/Ter33Design LLC

Cover art by Martin Johnson Heade, *Red Roses in a Japanese Vase on a Gold Velvet* (1850), public domain.

This is the first paperback edition.

Manufactured in the United States

ISBN: 979-8-9917990-1-0 (paperback)

"Unter einem fremden Himmel

Schatten Rosen

Schatten

Auf einer fremden Erde

zwischen Rosen und Schatten

in einem fremden Wasser

mein Schatten."

—Ingeborg Bachmann

"The most beautiful thing in the world is,

of course, the world itself."

—Wallace Stevens

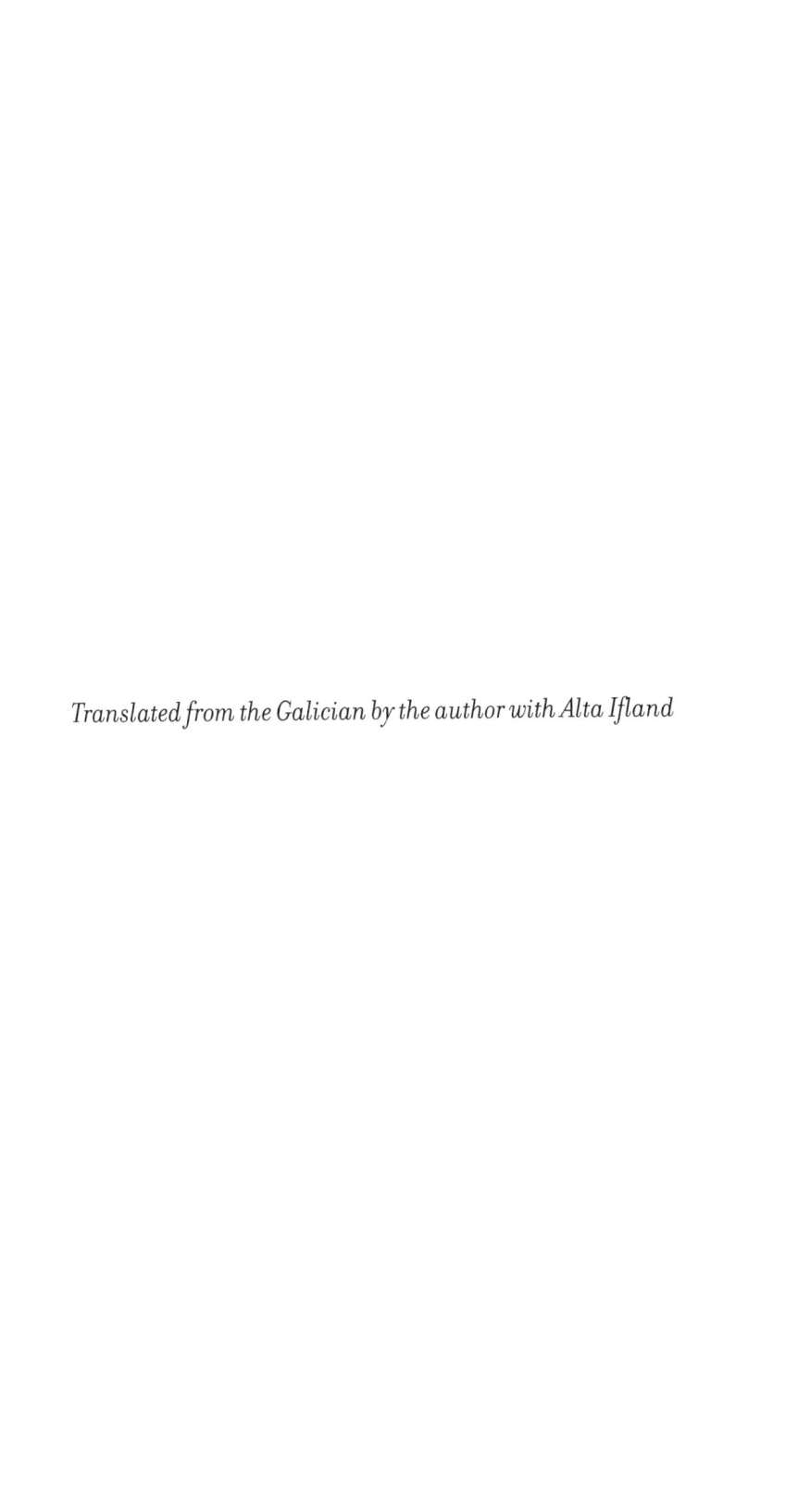

Translated from the Galician by the author with Alta Ifland

From *Acaso o inverno*, 2001

To get used to a language revealed

by cold.

To days where love only knows

the torn betrayal of abandonment

that preceded these words.

Because your speech faded away.

Trembling blue, mirror,

breaking towline, stagnant waters,

mirror in the night, cold gazes

halted in fear,

in your vestige.

Roughness settled between your shadows.

The experience of winter

like a passage of bitter roses.

Of oblivion.

Like a word reserved only

for pain.

April 1922 for C.P. Cavafy

Friezes of snakes, burnt saltpeter,

splendor of foam ravaged by time.

No one will return from Alexandria.

No one will get lost in that tumult

of withered iodine-colored manes,

of leaves buried under the sand.

The Attic pain of the gaunt walls,

the memory, like a feverish prayer,

the noise inflamed by tears.

No one will return from Alexandria.

The voices of lime, the fiery docks,

the starry race of prophets.

There too his dream passed

with the astonishment and ecstasy of forgotten days.

To end in a tremendous uproar of empty names.

No one will return from Alexandria.

Saying goodbye to the garlands of yesteryear

perhaps will sharpen a little more

the shadow enlarged by so much disaffection.

To confuse the days, to rest our breath

on another artifice, on other hours,

to avoid the flow of our aged blood.

No one will know

the sad passion that revealed

flowers of phosphorus, panoplies of ash.

No one will return from Alexandria.

From *O que ardeu nos espellos*, 2005

Trümmersprache[1]

of that

of the impossible return

of the impossible return and the debased days

of the impossible return and the debased days and the cold's forms

shaped for us

speaking of it

of the impossible return

and the ashen mouths

of the ashen mouths and the unbridgeable crack

where the world is lost and named

speaking of the wave that set us on fire with silence

of the wave that set us on fire with silence

and the psalm of snow

of the wave and the psalm of snow and the anchorless words

thrown into us

of that

of the mirror in which

we lost our faces

a long time ago

---

[1] Trümmersprache is a neologism created by the author, which combines two German words that could be translated as "language of the rubble."

of the mirror

we lost our faces

a long time ago

and the dawn of other days

like a soured and strange taste

of disappearance

speaking

of the impossible return and the dead mirrors

of the opaque mirrors

of this,

of this absent face

of that

Shores

The house we inhabit and the greyness left today;

the masks of ash, the confusion that precedes us.

And within that silence, quick foam

that sprouts on its shores.

The truth of the poem opening a crack in the world.

Like a wounded island. Like a shadow

that sinks into the mirrors and returns from them

with a trembling of wings and whiteness. Unrepeatable.

Revealing the secret gesture of the Sibyl.

Among the remote branches of winter,

an abyssal fire enveloping us,

a gaze of salt roses in the distance.

That revelation. A fluttering omen

over the devastated deltas of language.

In the end, a rewritten and burning sheet

against death. Against the simulacra of love

and its ruin. In the end, only

orderly emptiness. The same bewilderment.

A liminal territory without metaphor.

The bay where there is no rest for those of us who depart.

Vous ou la mort

Let the light rise over the ferns
at dawn, a fervor of remote birds;
let a warm breath come, an air adorn
the winters' illness. Where hail does not reach
oblivion. Where on its banks
dahlias emerge like fires. A dream of chrysalis
growing in the shadows, a breath
stolen from mirrors. That search.
The secret hidden in Hans Memling's gazes:
fragile, far from blackness. Flowers of snow.
The trembling between two waters,
like crossing a garden of virgin angels.
Otherwise, faces of sulfur; if not,
worn-out colors. Vous ou la mort.

Stéphane Mallarmé Peered out from Behind this Silence

We cannot deny boredom, roses, vanity;

artifice, its variations: what hovers

between us and a desert of burning statues.

Greatness was no more than writing

an absence. Passionless, rootless.

Without a dream to rekindle some glow.

A room forever closed. We cannot deny nature damaged

on every page. Winter's image

lived here: a boring contemplation,

the remains of the world. We cannot deny

that silence thus weaves its shadows.

That, like an animal sensing its death,

we will remain in these schist enclosures

that language reserves for us. It hides us.

Cassandra

Rumor of cymbals, wind, uprooted myrtles

winter moors, bell towers in smoke, shadows

cardinal lights, blackness of roses

glances of schist, burnt crests

falling rain, silence, fright,

its traps, old turmoil of grape bunches, bulbs

soot, broken statues, glaucous voices, salt forests

snowed expanse, Mandelstam-language

scratched night shores, food for the recumbent

snakes, woodworm, calcium branches

honeysuckle, ancient altarpieces, ships, rust

stagnant stories, Berlin, glebes of fire

the blue color of clay, pain, the stoned majesty

of pain, the devoured sarabande of their faces

broken columns of the world, fields of flax

September fields, fire of sleeping chrysalises

worn names, opals, almond-scented synagogues

crackling resins, ice spurts

the shuddering solitude of hospices, Poland, wounded beds

belvederes, soft waters of yesteryear, blossoming mouths

of blooming ash, burning days, ivy, surrendered chalices

women with unbridled hair, petitions for lime

swarthy eyes, the fields' stillness, last laurels

torn paradise, burning

we.

Aphorisms

A shadow animal complains among us:
someone is naming the disappearance.

Birds of white fire, of dead snow, are crossing the skies,
the sad days, others, of your father in the world.

Nobody knows the taste of identity,
only a dream of blind scribes, burning.

What light licks your anonymous face,
what cold woodworm is held within this oblivion?

The depth of mirrors, the hard path of glances,
a confusing story, that beating against them.

What rose amidst ancient waves of dread,
what never lay in your past.

All are fragments of the fall, of its pain
voices, pages.

From *Sombras rosas sombras*, 2008

Uprooting

i

Now, when winter leans over the hours
like a wounded gargoyle, when words emerge
from their old, hard bodies and the glances between us
are like an opaque tongue, like basalt ships
falling asleep, already lost; now, then,
when the shores of worn-out silence sink, in the end,
now, do you believe in the gentleness of mirrors,
in the harsh cold of the day.
The distance between those shadows
and disaffection.

ii

This language is a wasteland, this language
is the remains of an ancient cold, of a cold before
all cold. This language is Byzantium, flooded
with ornaments, birds of prey crossing fires,
water pouring with the stupor of despair.

This language is a house frozen like a shadow,

the names of the real, an angel losing his way;

this language is all that, the trembling light of a white sun,

a winter sun, verses turned back at the end

of Rilke's eighth elegy, verses that speak of a new ending,

of a new time, this language, this language is all that

a new time like great, abandoned *gares*[2],

the strange contour of flavors stranded in hard salt.

This language is a cloister for breath,

wounded hands that offer themselves no longer.

---

[2] gares – stations (in French in the original)

New Song for Simeon

"My life is light, waiting for the death wind,
like a feather on the back of the hand
dust in sunlight and memory in corners
wait for the wind that chills towards the dead land."
—T.S. Eliot

Who at night slowly seeks
shelter from the chaos and remains watching, serene,
how the desert grows with a siege
of white fire, how the city
raises friezes of shadow and trembling
over there; who awaits the cunning
of the hoarsest voices and, nevertheless,
places, once again, a candle
for his world, real roses
for that thirst, for chance; who,
if the mere dimness of an autumn light
lays down old ashes on pages of dreams,
travels even beyond the cold and carefully closes
his rooms and thus discovers
the deaf whiteness of the approaching silence.

Capitulation

someone quivered from the poem's truth

someone dreamed of the southern islands

someone resisted the blow of usury

someone sensed the sordidness of days

someone retraced yesterday's steps

someone left through waves of cold

someone rejected his face in the mirror

Stillleben [3]

"Austria, Bernhard, Contaxio

Thomas Bernhard, a Dor

a Enfermidade, Bernhard

Fracaso, Grünkrantz, Bernhard

Hochgobernitz, Inferno . . ."

—*Lois Pereiro*

The frozen hand stopped

on an impossible page;

the voices of stone,

the black splendor.

The titans holding up the world,

a whirlwind of burning wings

of birds reborn against the sky

(a trembling wall).

The stale, shattered air

of a synagogue, the ornaments

of dispossession, the blue crystal of pain.

Our prisons, the cloaks of winter,

the markets' humble, tarnished

[3.] Stillleben is German for "still life."

lamps. The alleys,

the secret dust of theaters.

Inscrutable rooms no one has entered . . .

The bygone illness of cafés.

Faces like shipwreck. Centuries of fear,

of thirst. Of fall:

the empty madness of time.

Here.

After Hugo von Hofmannsthal

And with silent eyes we grow from within

we, who understand nothing:

we grow, we depart

and other shadows pass by this shore.

And the season brings rain that will become

a gift to the world, and words, words like sad fruit

hit the skin of the falling night and nothing

but the dust of those afternoons remains to be forgotten.

And the age spheres roll like a dark wind

and, again, then, we lift our breath

from our roots, slowly, knowing that we are tired

finally surrendering.

Disappearances. Paraphrase of Nelly Sachs

under that skin, the song of the poisoned

under that sky, a wounded map

under the waters, the city of infamy

under the faces, a silent thirst

under the roses, the world crying.

What lies beneath skin and shadow

the promise of fire, the engraving of the living,

what you await like a full moon

of wild powder,

what you conjure with the will of the hungry;

what lies beneath the burned voice,

beneath the wound of age, beneath the tarnished mirrors;

what you name like the blank page,

like the saved rose, like the yearning hands;

what lies beneath days

and silence.

Under the Bridges Poets Shudder

The heart that descended into the depths of dawn,

the heart that burned in the destroyed pavane of the world,

the heart that advanced towards disappearance

the heart behind its shadow, against itself.

Under the bridges poets shudder

and you wanted to name that heart today as well

you wanted to say, like a dying secret,

the name of the dark city or the place where you hide

the candle and the fury of your restless days.

That heart with the taste of fermented daily bread

that heart against the perverse pomp of old age,

that heart filled with renewed passion for the chalice

that heart like a ship in the wounded light of time.

Under the bridges poets shudder,

old heroes whistle a ballad of flesh and bones

and you'd like to flee, burying your face in the morning

you'd like to hurt your tired hands now in another mirror.

Steine der Erinnerung[+]

You keep the curly lock and your parents' candle,

the old cloth

and a flower of ashes standing in for your lineage:

you keep the open books as a seal of this fire

as a sign of the humble ones

as a vivid alert against any surrender;

you keep the image of another winter,

the wheel of words murmured one by one

the shadow engulfing it: the stain of the damned.

[+] German for "Stones of Remembrance"

From *Arte de fuga*, 2015

Tears, Caravaggio

"Coral dust. Anabasis."

—John Ash

Now, in Porto Ercole,

outside the prisons of the world,

days hurt like cold rust.

This season pours out its thirst,

vine leaves trembling in your hands,

the fruit of the blood no one bites into.

The warm, scarlet hair you

sought at dusk hurts;

the Tyrian purple glow in other eyes,

in condemned bodies.

Dirty beds at dawn,

amaranth lanterns of the feasts,

stains of shadow, golden clarity

of your manly dream.

Now in this summer that is slowly rotting

days hurt like salt

(a curse devouring the gazes

of the one you loved most):

The indigo wind of those lost days,

a scent of powder and silver.

Where was the warm, purple heart

of sublime autumns

a blind flower will slowly grow for you,

a hawthorn like an omen.

Quietly, you sought in twilight

the most beautiful ochres of Emmaus bread,

A gesture's light in a mystery of clay;

but you will no longer call upon the angel

to grant you his cry

nor will you rest your breath

with the same gentleness as the sea in the background.

Now in Porto Ercole,

you remember, exhausted, the paths of exile,

the crimson walls of the leper colonies,

the faces of the drowned,

the phosphorus of voices deploring your name,

the color of your anger.

Paradise

The childhood light no longer trembles
like a quick star at the far end of the room,
our humble rose is no longer sensed
in the cold of the world, in the dark city.
From each object, its time will grow
and your body will walk on other maps.
Ships are no longer leaving with new dreams,
There are no quiet books for your thirsty gaze.
No deep footprints, no voices taking you away
and no music to dispel fears.
Life's dark season was real
out there, they said your name without speaking of angels or crowns.
There was no farewell, and no diary was written.
This is what your days are made of:
from the same word
where paradise ended.

Someone Alive Passes by

"Get up and walk through the city of the massacre, [5]
and with your hand touch and lock your eyes"
—Hayim Nahman Bialik
> *In memory of Jaime Vándor, survivor*

Where does this wind take us through the city
on fire still, your city on fire?

To the large theatres, perhaps?

To those nocturnal butterflies no longer awake
in the old, closed bookstore?

To the corridors wrapped in voices
and mauve light
like forgotten dew?

Where to go?

To those streets, humiliated at their roots,

---

5. From the poem "In the City of Slaughter," translated by Vladimir Jabotinsky.

smelling of gas and old salt,

where the secret of the world

was once written?

—the animal of pain carved in jade awaits,

lurking in your dream:

Barcarolle, cooling in your mouth, a sad taste.

Where, without you, where?

(The cold pavane will slowly go on in palaces,

perhaps theatre sets, Bruckner's thunder,

crumbling stucco . . .)

To whom does this wind speak?

There is hardly anything left in the drawers

and the memory of love, like dead bread,

was ruined once and for all.

Where are we going, where?

Because the snow visits every door

and already your name, Shulamit,

tears off this poem like sick skin.

Old Masters

The theme, slowly invoking the Angelus,

is printed in hidden scores

and in that silent, minor poem

written by Zbigniew Herbert

as a quiet homage.

The theme of the frost on the humble, worn-out boards

of the mornings of the world.

There is no signature, no pride,

there is hardly any certainty:

hands resting on old aromas of clay.

The perfection of silence is thus described

like the anonymous scribe

tracing a winter scene

among Venetian manuscripts

between candles and cloths of rarefied smoke.

Should neglect enter the parents' house like a disease,

may their shrinking hearts

be covered by oblivion

(the deep lament of that psalm in exile)

that is the purpose, the task torn away

from shadows: an illuminated Virgin,

a mortal's gaze in a mirror.

The same workshop where in the evenings

one smells the wet cinnamon of paint,

voices like stagnant water;

the fear of men in the night

in silent cities the color of Siena

The season announcing the stars,

the leaves' whiteness in the apple trees:

all this, a vision beyond fear.

Always beside a river that, like cold silk, flows away.

A Reading of W. G. Sebald

A beach of bones on the northern borders
and the memory of Napoleonic blue pomp
lost; a hall of dead steps at the heart
of the cold, filigrees of time with its dark fire
seeping between faces and masks.
The memory of the moors like an animal fleeing
through each winter still trembles
in the Kreutzer sonata, in the purple bonfires of dawn.
Old stamps eaten away by the salt of time,
the defeated lineages, a crash of noble porcelain.
The statues' gazes after the rondeaux,
the Carbonari flags against the skies of Europe,
the archives of battles, the candle lit in exile.

Story of Isaac

"He said, 'I've had a vision
And you know I'm strong and holy
I must do what I've been told"
—Leonard Cohen

Tell me, what new spell or sacrifice
will those wounded hands of yours accept, tell me;
What message has caught
in the worn-out heart of the world,
what waters are flowing now
between my dream and your failure
like a defeated god,

When you open those doors
there will remain between us nothing but a steppe,
the hardened and recurrent corbel of other days,
only an angel's shadow
beyond our words.

Tell me how to know the sordid chrysalis
of all the words,

the gestures of weariness before our cold mouths;

How to recompose, then,

the torn fragments of this gaze?

When you open those doors

only a profile of poor roses will remain

and my breath will already rest on other maps,

far away.

When you come to find me,

you will find only the ashes

foretold by the prophets,

the silence of fruits protected by no one.

Tell me, what weapons of ice still await us,

what renunciation has been woven and unwoven

irremediably in this lineage,

what tides have separated us forever

from the roots of this dead house?

Gold like Frozen Fire

In the firmness of the stone heart rooted in time

and in the cold of the green algae with which the waters name

each generation; in the porticos of the wind crossed by eagles,

in the rains sowing words of bronze, without usury

—there we'll find the secret of days, an old root—

by the colors of the sanguine smoke leaving their breath:

in the carvings of the vigilant Romanesque animals, in the footprints

between the walls, in the ambers slowly carved by hands,

in the water roses sprouting to testify

—for them, a light will come alive when we look over the rivers—

in the sea of ferns that raises its dark wave in the valleys,

in the pearly silences of winters, in the boreal voices

like shiny wolves, exhausted, fleeing in the night,

in the iridescent tail of a centaur crossing alone in battle—

wherever they are, the helplessness of life, the steps on the rivers'

stones—

in the pages written with the commotion of the undying days

in the figures born from limestone, from the craft of splendor,

like a miniaturized, secret task:

in the fruits preserving their essence, the pulse, the resins

—it hits them with the breath blowing again on their faces —

in the corollas of tears woven like snow for the absent

(someone alone in the corridors, oblivion like soot on love)

and in the prayer whispered for them with a taste of whiteness,

and in the autumn's old oboes kissing the earth's crust

—the story of us inhabits that silence: an infinite vision of salt—

in the paths of life where breath is ruined and, nevertheless,

continues, in the country flooded like an ancient shipwreck,

in the wind extinguishing the remains of failure,

so that we may break down pain, which hinders our sight, like ash,

so that we may throw an anchor that keeps us on this shore,

so that we may save the earth's heart trembling behind us

—words of shadows, gold like frozen fire.

From *Ese tépedo vento que pasa sobre o mundo*, 2019

Prelude

You will feel the waves you will feel the blue wind

the waves returning

you will feel the foam of an unfathomable sea

hitting your burning

free body

you will hear the purple clamor of the seasons

passing voices birds announcing

summer sweetly summer at your side

you will sense words white as the first light of the world

you will slowly sense

how the roses offer the secret of their days

you will feel a foreboding inside you

a river crossing the dream that you had forgotten in the shadow

you will smell the fierce aroma of all that

of all that will be loved forever

with that definitive dedication of those crowned by life

of everything sleepless that feeds

the dance

the colors of the stars still pure

you will thus feel it

walking beyond time

of its worn maps

beyond

leaving behind all the deserts

all useless vanity

you will feel your face maturing in the mirrors

the trembling of that other skin

that no one had yet managed to move

the night

you will feel the night like a beautiful sanctuary

of silences

the earth sown from your clean heart

the free blood in your saved hands

in that warm mouth that in the end will forget

the terror

the barren territory of so much abandonment so much

that's how you will feel

the fire lit up all around you

that's how

that's how you will feel the seas split like in an old prophecy

you will feel all that

the petals healing from their ashes

a glow preserved in the depths of glances

disaffection overcome by fury

you will feel next to you

the imminence of rain foretold

for a long time

you will feel your breath

in another breath that welcomes you

that welcomes you without limits or expectations

you will feel that nothing was useless despite the darkest waters

that nothing will be lost with tears

with the wind

you will feel

that everything celebrates the inexhaustible line of the horizon.

We are the Countries

"Die Wüste wächst: weh, wer zur Wüste ward!"
—Friedrich Nietzsche

"We are the real countries, not the boundaries drawn on maps
with the names of powerful men"
—Michael Ondaatje

We are the countries, not the worn-out,
forgotten borders,
where the wind no longer sows the days.
The desert advances, the desert advances outside,
but we are the bodies that will resist it,
we are the bodies that will cross the rivers,
that will await the atrocious onslaught of time.
Because we are the countries,
those footprints that speak
of ferns rising before the fire,
the warm matter of the moved voices,
of the nights without ruin.
The desert advances,
the word trembles like a cold rose,

but we are the countries, the true land

where lovers leave behind silence and terror.

We are the countries,

not the cymbals announcing defeat.

We are the glances emerging from tears,

dreaming of springs, closing the wounds

of other hands cracked by the hostile darkness of the world.

We are the place of a deeper, shared root;

We will erase the line of ashes, we will go beyond the dead snow.

The desert advances,

hard sand incessantly stings

the hearts of children, the high towers of this blood,

but we come from the margins to drop anchor here,

to stop the gale and the end, the disappointment.

Because we are the countries,

not the scorched harvest,

not the dying tongue of the animals of sadness,

never the caged breath of the shipwrecked.

We remain calm before the desert and its black wave,

we are the bodies that held themselves up, flags,

we are flags in the vortex of the dance and the clamor.

We are the countries, we are the bodies,

the countries that will rise again from the shadows.

It is not Madness this Beauty

"If love be not in the house there is nothing"
—*Ezra Pound*

It is not madness this beauty resting on the world
Although ruin and ashes now surround your breath.
The hidden work of days, the bronze light in Ravenna,
generations of goldsmiths who spoke in God's tongues,
that made roses of fire grow from timeless clay.
What was not a mistake was not a dark mirror in the night.
No, the battle against the hosts of death and desert
was not in vain. It will not be a poem devoured by oblivion.
Shipwrecked in the hearts of yesterday's ladies, those
who look out from the hidden frescoes of galleries
and rooms covered in splendor and worn gems:
What will become of this house if love does not live in it?
What will become of the sibyl's song dreamed by minstrels?
Skin bristling with the dawn and the fury of passion and chaos,
Bianca de Medici's mouth lined with fine coral.
Beauty is not madness even if palaces collapse,
faces were not sculpted with anxiety and fear,
eyes mottled with the silence of rotten fruit,

the hands of the lute player did not grow cold in the dense night.

Those words will not be clamor, perishing in darkness.

From *Trono e caléndula*, 2023

After us

We thought that the days were ending

like lost, old rivers,

but this beauty and the colors of the world

will continue tomorrow, will continue

when our steps are buried

by the sand and the tide

and in the bodies love remains barely

like the ashes of a sleeping star.

We thought that the words of fire

would not know other mouths,

that the most vivid gestures

would become salt, oblivion

after this farewell, after time darkening,

after the last traveled season.

But this language will rise again

the defeated heart, the house of yesteryear,

the ruin devoured by silence.

We thought that this land

would not give another gift,

that the nights would be a strange desert,

that that crazy fascination

would sink like an animal of jade,

like a wounded face of stone.

But the roses will continue

to be born like a miracle

and the wind will throw its seed,

the burning message

of all that returns.

Imminence of September

The warm memory

of the fruits we will no longer bite into,

the quietly fading colors,

like an aged sob,

the flow of words moving through us,

all of these trembled between bodies.

Birds pass by, shadows,

purple lights in a foretold goodbye;

we return inside, to the rooms of silence,

the night arrives like a sudden tide,

devouring the roses,

freezing the mouths of the absent.

The music of the days is a sky collapsing,

a border between lost summers

and forests the color of copper and sobs;

the music of the nights is a jasper bird,

waters advancing like a dense will,

like a siege of voices in the dust.

We shell the dormant seed,

We feel the butterflies of chalk and blue ash,

we have reached the heart of the earth,

we have reached September.

We remain in the dream and the longing.